T0193958

I BELIEVE

I Have Confidence in Myself, Just Like Rocky, the Musical Dog

Coloring and Activity Book 7

SUZANNE MONDOUX
Illustrated by Gaëtanne Mondoux

BALBOA.
PRESS

A DIVISION OF HAY HOUSE

Balboa Press books may be ordered through booksellers or by contacting:

Balboa Press
A Division of Hay House
1663 Liberty Drive
Bloomington, IN 47403
www.balboapress.com
1 (877) 407-4847

Print information available on the last page.

ISBN: 978-1-9822-2267-3 (sc)
ISBN: 978-1-9822-2280-2 (e)

Balboa Press rev. date: 02/22/2019

This book belongs to

_____

I am _____ years old

It was a quiet morning on the ranch. The first day of school had finally come. The new students would arrive soon. Jojo was preparing her class as the sun rose over the horizon.

The morning light shone brilliantly orange over the autumn colors. Trees of every color climbed the mountains surrounding the valley. She looked up at the birds flying overhead. In the distance she saw a dog walking towards the ranch. It would be her first student.

The clock struck 7:30 am. It was far too early. Class did not start until 9:00 am. She waited by the gate for the tiny dog with big ears flapping in the wind. The dog walked slowly towards her. By 7:40 am the dog had reached the gate.

"Good morning," said Jojo. "I am the teacher here at the ranch. Have you come to join us on the first day of school?" She opened the gate door for the dog.

"Good morning. My name is Rocky. This is my first day of school." Rocky looked up at the beautiful golden mare.

Before Rocky walked through the ranch gate the ground thundered beneath their feet. Behind him galloped Carlo and Teddy, the curious and adventurous horses. A long hard-shell case hung down from Carlo's back.

"Good morning," they shouted. "We have come to join Rocky on his first day at school."

Jojo opened the gate even wider. Rocky walked through slowly and quietly. Carlo and Teddy galloped through the gates like conquering heroes. They kicked up a bit of dust behind them and rose up on their hind legs neighing with joy.

Rocky jumped up on the bale of hay away from the flying hooves.

"Welcome back to the ranch," said Jojo. "We have not seen you since last winter. I am sure you have many stories to share of your adventures."

"Thank you. Yes, we have plenty of stories to share with everyone," said Teddy. "One of our great adventures was meeting Rocky. He can speak for himself. He is a great storyteller, great singer and songwriter. He writes his own music as well."

Rocky jumped off the bale of hay to approach Teddy.

"Welcome Rocky," said Jojo. "Tell me how you came to be at our ranch. Class does not begin until 9:00 am, so we have a bit of time to talk."

Rocky looked up at the three horses waiting for him to speak. He stepped a bit closer. He took a deep breath and looked across the field. He turned his gaze back up at the horses.

"I was in this place where there were no other dogs and lots of humans. I was left on my own all the time and I could not get out of my cage. Some of the days were very hot in the summer and it was cold most of the winter. To keep myself busy I wrote songs in my mind and imagined myself playing the guitar. I like the sound of the guitar.

"How did you come to learn to write music," asked Jojo.

"One day this very nice lady came up to my cage and told me not to be afraid. She said she would open the cage door and let me out. I was so happy I jumped right into her arms. I licked her face and barked and barked and barked with joy. She said she was from this place that rescues dogs from unpleasant circumstances. I did not understand what she meant by that. I had lived there in that cage my entire life." Rocky looked back out at the field as though he was looking for something or someone.

Jojo walked over to Rocky. "The other students will not be here for some time. Please go on."

"This nice lady, her name was Sophie, brought me to where there were lots of other dogs. I had never seen so many dogs before. They had this big yard to play in. It was not quite as big as this ranch but still very big. A few days after I arrived Sophie invited me to come with her for a day trip. She said I was going to meet a group of people who wanted to meet me. I had no idea where I was going. About thirty minutes of driving in the car we turned into a driveway. It was lined with manicured green trees and lots of flowers. I had never seen anything so beautiful. The car pulled up in front of a big blue house with white trim. My wet nose was pressed up against the car window. I looked out onto a large porch circling the front and sides of the house.

"Sophie opened the car door for me. I jumped out and followed her up the wooden steps. When I stepped onto the porch men and women with grey hair and wrinkled skin were sitting in rocking chairs. They looked down at me and smiled. They called out my name. They said they had been waiting for me all morning. One by one they got out of their chairs and followed Sophie and me inside the big blue house. Sophie told me we were in a home where older people come to live when they need help and cannot live on their own.

"Some of these older men and women were walking straight up, some were walking bent over like a question mark, some were walking with canes, some with a thing called a walker, and some were in what Sophie called a wheelchair. They followed us into this big room. Everyone took a seat and waited in silence. Sophie stood in the middle of the room and introduced me as Rocky, a rescue dog. It was not until Sophie took me home and I spent time with the other dogs that I learned I was a rescue dog and what that meant.

"I sat next to Sophie and wagged my tail. I was very happy and did not know why. All these people wanted to meet me. As the day went on I spent a bit of time with each person in the big blue house. Later in the day the older woman who was bent over like a question mark walked over to the piano. Another man in a wheelchair rolled himself next to the piano and reached for the guitar leaning next to the wall. Another woman took her cane and pushed the music books to the center of the table. Some of the books were distributed amongst everyone in the room. Some of the books had songs in them for people to read from. Then the music started. The singing went on and on while I traveled from lap to lap. Then I found myself sitting on the lap of the man in the wheelchair playing the guitar. Next to him was a music book. I sat with him until it was time go back home.

"The next day we returned to the big blue house. The man in the wheelchair was waiting for me on the porch. He took me in his arms and sat me on his lap and rolled us into the music room. He placed the guitar in his arms and rested the music book against the arm of his chair. He said to me, Rocky I will teach you how to read music and write your own songs. Each day I visited everyone in the big blue house. When I was done the man in the wheelchair come for me to continue my music lessons.

"Then one day when I arrived at the big blue house the man in the wheelchair was not waiting for me on the porch. When I walked through the house he was not there, and when I walked into the music room he was not there either. I ran to his bedroom and he was not there either. The room was empty. His things were not in the room.

"Sophie took me in her arm. She told me the man in the wheelchair had died. But she said he had left something for me. She carried me to the music room. The wheelchair was next to the guitar. A letter was left on the seat of the wheelchair addressed to 'Rocky'. I would like to read it to you."

Rocky removed the letter from his pouch. He sat on his hind legs and opened the letter.

"To my dear friend Rocky,

I am gone now. I know this will make you sad. It is ok if you cry and miss me. I will miss you as well. Your visits gave me lots of joy. Before I fell sick and became confined to this wheelchair I was a musician who traveled the world singing and playing the guitar for many people. I also had the honour of being a music teacher. It was such an honour to spend time with you teaching you about music.

I want you to know that you also taught me about music. You shared your story with me, which touched my heart. It would be my honour if you accepted this gift. I leave you my guitar and music books. I also know of a great teacher who will continue with your lessons. I have made the necessary arrangements for you to meet Jojo.

Not long ago I met these two great horses Carlo and Teddy in the wild field behind the house. Yes, I had some of the nurses take me back there from time to time and leave me to enjoy the beautiful wilderness. The horses and I talked for hours, and I told them about you. I asked them to do me a favor and they accepted.

You expressed on numerous occasions that you did not know if you were a good musician and songwriter. You did not know if you had or have the confidence to play guitar with other musicians and for others. I know you have what it takes to be a great musician. I believe in you, Rocky. Now you need to continue with your lessons and continue believing in yourself.

Your loving friend Bob (The old man in the wheelchair).

Rocky wiped his tears. He folded the letter and put it back in the pouch.

"So that is why Carlo is traveling with a guitar case on his back. I can only assume there is a guitar in there with your name on it, Rocky," said Jojo.

"Yes," said Rocky. "That is my guitar."

Carlo removed the guitar from his back and gave it to Rocky. Rocky placed it on the bale of hay.

"When was the last time you played guitar, sang a song, or wrote a song," asked Jojo.

"I don't know," said Rocky.

Jojo took the guitar and walked towards the barn with it. "Come, follow me."

The three of them followed Jojo into the barn.

"Look up here Rocky," she pointed to a poster on the wall. "We are having a winter music festival here at the ranch. You have three months to prepare.

Rocky glared up at the poster and Jojo. "But, I..."

Jojo looked into his eyes. "Rocky, there is no but here."

She handed the guitar back to Rocky. "Together we will help you become more confident so you can discover who Rocky really is. You are more than just your music, Rocky, and together we will unravel this mystery. And together we will discover what you are capable of as a musician, guitar player, songwriter and singer. But I only ask one thing of you."

"Yes, what is that," said Rocky.

"You accept the challenge of believing in yourself," she said.

Teddy nudged his leg against Rocky. "We traveled weeks with you to get here. We can stay here with you to help you, if you wish for us to stay. But we will not miss this winter music festival for anything. You will make new friends at the ranch. The first day of school is exciting and fun! I know you are nervous and worried of what the others will think and say about you, but they are worried and thinking the same things as you. Just be yourself and you will see that everything will turn out ok."

Rocky smiled and looked out the barn door. He glanced out into the field.

"Are you expecting someone?" said Jojo.

Rocky looked up at the horses. "When I was writing songs with the man in the wheelchair I wrote about other dogs out there who need rescuing. I know they would love to come to the ranch or have a family like I did with Sophie. I was sad when I said goodbye to Sophie to come here with Carlo and Teddy. But I am happy for the home she gave me.

Maybe I can continue to write songs about other animals who need our help."

"That's a great idea," said Jojo. "You are here for as long as you need to be. We will take it one day at a time. Sophie will continue taking care of other dogs and other animals. It is your time to become the Rocky you dream of being. You can help Sophie and everyone else who help animals through your music."

"It sounds like you are saying that my music has purpose. That my music is not only to make me happy and others happy, sing and dance but have greater purpose by helping others in ways I may not yet see or understand!" Rocky reached for his guitar and rubbed his paw against the strings.

He stood up tall and smiled.

"That's right," said Jojo. "There is meaning in what you do. How does that make you feel?

Rocky looked up at the poster. "The meaning, the purpose for my music gives me great confidence. I feel different about this now. I give a new meaning to my music. When can we begin with the lessons?"

Carlo, Teddy and Jojo smiled and laughed. "Very soon, the school bell is about to ring. Here come the other students."

Rocky practiced everyday and prepared for the winter music festival. For the first 30 days of school he tinkered and played around with other musical instruments. He listened to others play different musical instruments and then he created a musical group for the winter music festival.

Rocky would love to hear you play a musical instrument and hear the songs you have written.

For the next 30 days

- Write a song

- Play a musical instrument for 30 minutes a day

- Learn how to write your own music, and

- Write a song on how your music can help animals

Let your imagination take you anywhere it wants to take you!

Lets begin.

Most importantly - Have fun!

Remember to smile.

Remember to laugh.

Remember to be curious and ask questions.

Remember to Believe in yourself.

Say out loud 10 times.

I Believe in myself.
I Believe in myself.
I Believe in myself.
I Believe in myself.
I Believe in myself.
I Believe in myself.
I Believe in myself.
I Believe in myself.
I Believe in myself.
I Believe in myself.

Day 1

_____

_____

_____

_____

_____

_____

_____

_____

_____

_____

_____

_____

Day 2

_____

_____

_____

_____

_____

_____

_____

_____

_____

_____

_____

_____

_____

Day 3

Day 4

_____

_____

_____

_____

_____

_____

_____

_____

_____

_____

_____

_____

_____

Day 5

_____

_____

_____

_____

_____

_____

_____

_____

_____

_____

_____

_____

Day 6

Day 7

Day 8

_____

_____

_____

_____

_____

_____

_____

_____

_____

_____

_____

_____

_____

Day 9

_____

_____

_____

_____

_____

_____

_____

_____

_____

_____

_____

_____

Day 10

_____

_____

_____

_____

_____

_____

_____

_____

_____

_____

_____

_____

_____

Day 11

_____

_____

_____

_____

_____

_____

_____

_____

_____

_____

_____

_____

_____

Day 12

_____

_____

_____

_____

_____

_____

_____

_____

_____

_____

_____

_____

_____

Day 13

_____

_____

_____

_____

_____

_____

_____

_____

_____

_____

_____

_____

Day 14

Day 15

Day 16

_____

_____

_____

_____

_____

_____

_____

_____

_____

_____

_____

_____

_____

_____

Day 17

Day 18

_____

_____

_____

_____

_____

_____

_____

_____

_____

_____

_____

_____

_____

Day 19

_____

_____

_____

_____

_____

_____

_____

_____

_____

_____

_____

_____

Day 20

_____

_____

_____

_____

_____

_____

_____

_____

_____

_____

_____

_____

Day 21

Day 22

_____

_____

_____

_____

_____

_____

_____

_____

_____

_____

_____

_____

_____

Day 23

_____

_____

_____

_____

_____

_____

_____

_____

_____

_____

_____

_____

_____

Day 24

Day 25

_____

_____

_____

_____

_____

_____

_____

_____

_____

_____

_____

Day 26

Day 27

_____

_____

_____

_____

_____

_____

_____

_____

_____

_____

_____

_____

Day 28

_____

_____

_____

_____

_____

_____

_____

_____

_____

_____

_____

_____

_____

_____

Day 29

_____

_____

_____

_____

_____

_____

_____

_____

_____

_____

_____

_____

Day 30

WOW! YOU ARE AMAZING!!!!!!!!!!!!!!!

YOU DID ALL THE FUN STUFF!

YOU PARTICIPATED IN 30 DAYS OF FUN!

KEEP GOING!

EXPLORE YOUR IMAGINATION!

BELIEVE IN YOURSELF ALWAYS!

SHARE THE SONGS YOU WROTE ABOUT ANIMALS,
HOW YOUR MUSIC CAN HELP ANIMALS, AND THE
EXPLORATION OF YOUR IMAGINATION WITH A FRIEND!

THANK YOU FOR BEING GOOD AND
KIND TO EVERY ANIMAL.

On behalf of all the ANIMALS – thank you for
making this a better world for ALL OF US!

Printed in the United States
By Bookmasters